/50

Foot-Ball:

Its History for Five Centuries

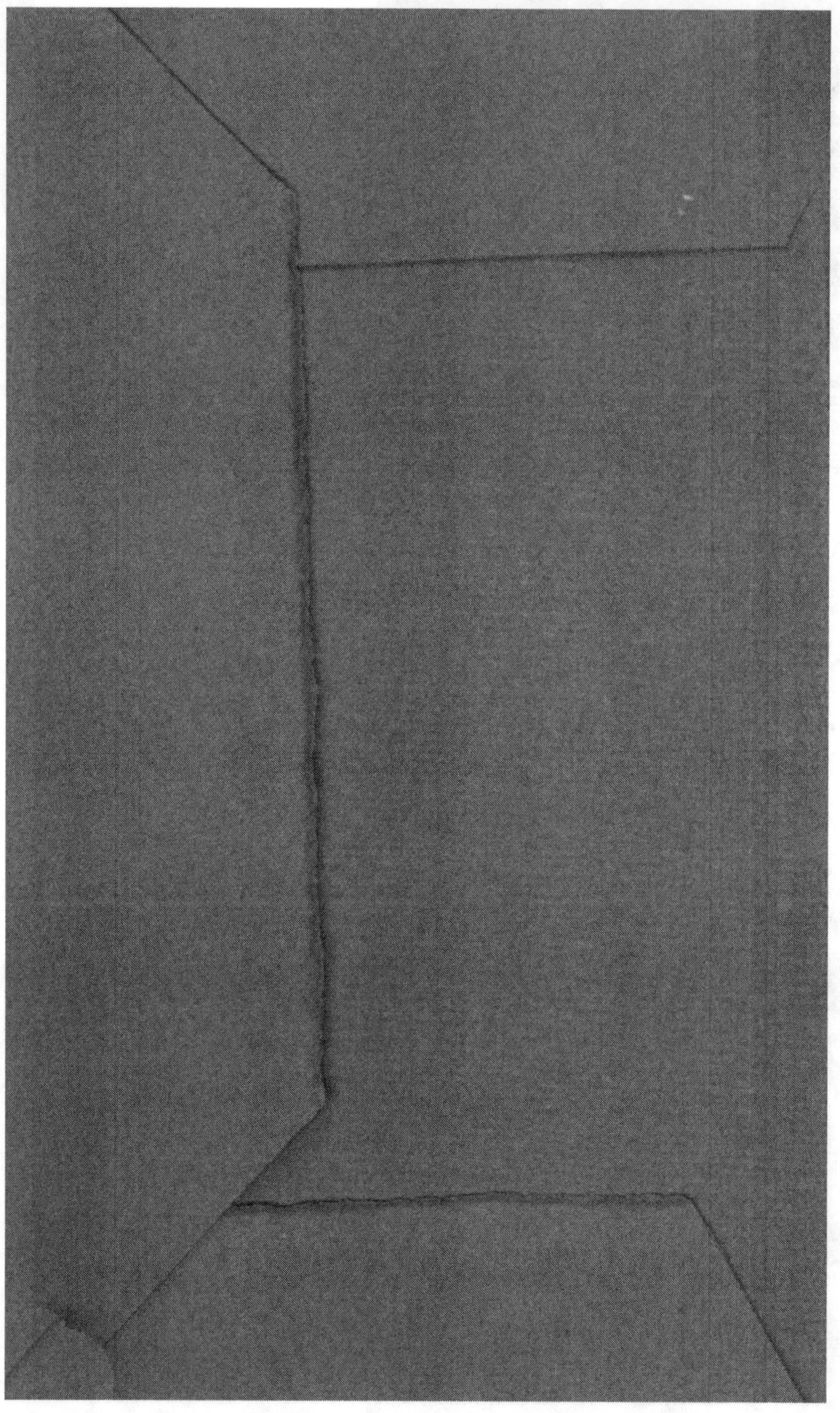

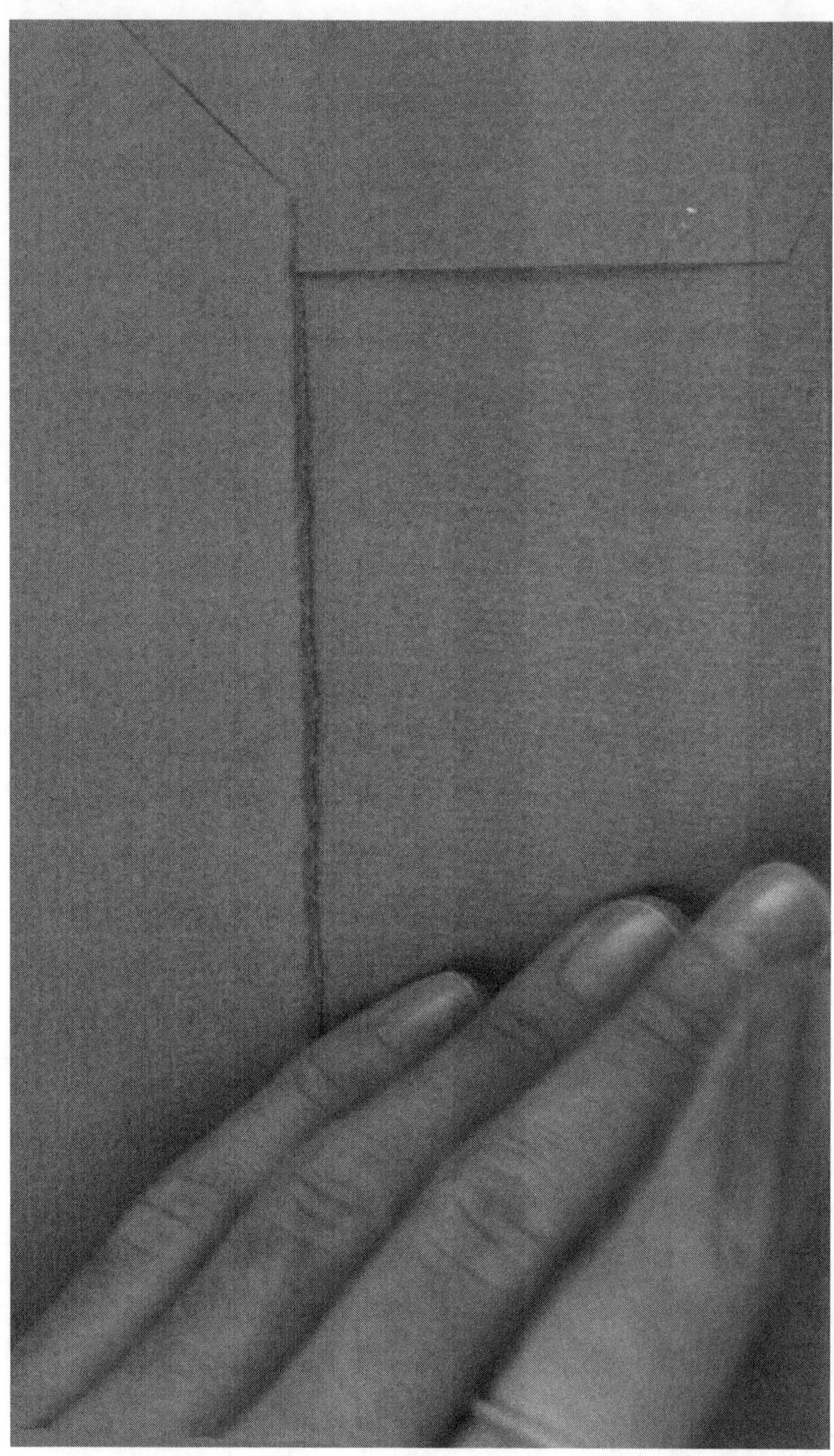

Foot-Ball:

Its History for Five Centuries

BY

MONTAGUE SHEARMAN

AND

JAMES E. VINCENT.

LONDON:
Field & Tuer, The Leadenhall Press, E.C.
Simpkin, Marshall & Co.; Hamilton, Adams & Co.

FIELD & TUER,
THE LEADENHALL PRESS, E.C.
T 4,192.

Preface.

HE Authors, who welcome this opportunity of addressing their readers through the conventional channel of a preface, have not written without an object. That object has not been to teach the art of football, which art can only be attained by practice. It has been to collect the scattered and fragmentary knowledge which surrounds the history of an ancient pastime. In the pursuit of this object they have performed the pleasant duty of exploring many literary storehouses, and have not seldom been compelled to wander far out of the beaten track. They will have attained their object if they can pass on to their readers one-tenth of the delight which resulted to themselves from their wanderings. There also resulted a

theory, which was not adopted without anxious argument, that the games of football now in vogue owe their origin almost entirely to the public schools; and that in the public schools rules were the consequence of circumstances and environment. At the same time football has a history which has been faithfully followed.

In addition to the thanks, which we cannot adequately express, to ancient authors, we owe a debt of gratitude to Walter Rye, Esq., than whom none is better versed in the antiquities of sport, for valuable advice as to sources of information.

M. SHEARMAN.
J. E. VINCENT.

Contents.

CHAPTER I.

The Origin of Football.

HEN a national taste or a national trait is under consideration, sound criticism often falls from a foreign observer. At the present day an American novelist, whose subtle analysis of character is charming English readers, has pronounced his opinion that an Englishman is only to be understood and appreciated when he is seen out of doors in a flannel suit ; while a French critic goes further, and assigns a narrower sphere to British ability, by making the observation that an Englishman is only perfectly happy when he has a ball to play with. Certain it is, that, good as they are in any branch of sport, it is in games in which a ball of any kind is used that the members of the English race are the most enthusiastic and proficient players.

There is another feature, too, in such games which renders them peculiarly interesting; they have all an ancient and an honourable history. So far back indeed does the history of the different kinds of ball-play reach, that the investigation of their origin, and for the present in particular of the earliest records of the game of football, can hardly fail to produce interesting fruit.

The most learned historian of sports and pastimes, Joseph Strutt, indulges in an elaborate antiquarian inquiry into the origin of the ball, having recourse to the most ancient of the classics for his authorities. Hand-ball, he says, is, "if Homer may be accredited, coeval at least with the destruction of Troy. Herodotus attributes the invention of the ball to the Lydians; succeeding writers have affirmed that a female of distinction named Anagalla, a native of Corcyra, was the first who made a ball for the purposes of pastime, which she presented to Nausica (*sic*), the daughter of Alcinous, King of Phæacia, and at the same time taught her how to use it." To emphasize his authority, the antiquary quotes three lines from "Pope's Odyssey (bk. v.).

> " O'er the green mead the sporting virgins play,
> Their shining veils unbound, along the skies,
> Tost and retost, the ball incessant flies."

The same author is much, and it would seem somewhat unnecessarily, distressed at the fact that the writer of a 14th century manuscript preserved in Trinity College, Oxford, and the Venerable Bede are not in harmony as to the early capacities of the athletic saint, Cuthbert. The former says of him that "he pleyde atte balle with the children that his fellowes were," while the latter merely makes mention of his general excellence at games involving great muscular exertion. The plain fact of the matter is, that the origin of the ball is one of those matters which must of necessity be lost in antiquity. Nature herself supplies an endless variety of balls of all sizes, suitable for throwing from hand to hand, and the act of playing with them is instinctive. The apple and the orange are, so to speak, objects which nature supplies, not only as objects of food, but also as materials for pastime ; clay, too, and snow, are of so plastic a nature that the hands even of children naturally mould them into a spherical form and hurl them to and fro in sport.

Before, however, an attempt be made to show how the game of football became developed as a specific sport, it is without doubt the duty of sober historians first to chronicle the legends which have attached themselves to the foundation of the game. Firstly, it is said that in ancient times it was the custom to kick a large stone from parish to parish, both in Scotland and in England, for the purpose of marking boundaries and asserting rights of way; and that in this practice, which was indulged in by large bodies of the parishioners, each of whom desired to give his kick when he got the opportunity, we are to find the origin of football. Certain it is, at any rate, that the practice of kicking a leather football over a path on Whit-Monday, for the purpose of exercising a right of way, endured into the present century in the Isle of Purbeck in Dorsetshire, a ball being annually presented to the workmen of certain quarries for that purpose. But the origin of the practice, both in that locality and in some other parts of the country where it is known to have been followed, is shrouded in antiquity; and there is little evidence to show that this practice caused the rise of football, instead of having arisen at a time when the game itself was well known. This latter view seems the most probable. The second legend of the origin of the game is one of a gruesome character, and far more suitable to be chronicled in connection with the legendary or mythical stage of history. The ancient Teutons, it is averred, did not scalp the bodies of their slaughtered

enemies (as did the Choctaws), nor did they muti-
late them (as do the Bashi-bazouks), but in grim
sport cut off their heads and kicked them about,
after the fashion of the Baron in the Ingoldsby
legend of Sheppey, who, after he had donned the
famous boots, first killed the holy father with a
magnificent "punt," and afterwards encompassed
his own ruin by an ill-timed "place-kick" at the
skull of Grey Dolphin. But even granting that
our savage progenitors indulged in the amiable
pastime which we have described (and after all
it is far from improbable), we can still comfort
ourselves by feeling certain that football had no
such horrible origin ; for the game of head-kicking
may have been magnificent—may have been
superb (to quote the famous *mot*), but it certainly
was not football. It is curious, however, that
amongst the traditions of the city of Chester,
which is one of the oldest homes of the game,
where it was played by all the inhabitants of the
town on the Roodee, the head of a Dane is still
stated to have been the original ball used in the
game. Perhaps it is best to give these two
legends, as in duty bound, and then to pass on
to matters which are of unquestioned historical
accuracy. Indeed, were it not for these legends,
it would seem obvious that the foot-ball, as dis-

tinguished from the hand-ball, was the product of civilization and invention. Such indeed it seems to have been in fact, although it must be confessed that the subjoined explanation of the origin of the foot-ball is in part hypothetical and based upon *à priori* grounds. It is probable that the first foot-ball was the Roman *follis,* or inflated bladder, of which Martial speaks when he advises boys and old men alike to play it. But the *follis* was, primarily at least, a hand-ball; and a bladder was probably used first for that purpose, for the simple reason that it was able, on account of its lightness, to be struck into the air with the hand without pain, and with ease. At some uncertain but momentous date, an impetuous player must, after missing the ball with his hand, have kicked out petulantly with his sandalled foot, and so unconsciously made the first experiment in the art of drop-kicking, or punting. Swiftly and strongly the ball flew, farther than it could be cast by the strongest arm or smitten by the lustiest hand; and this must inevitably have been the first step to the later development of the game played with the *follis,* when it was kicked with the foot or struck with the hand at discretion and convenience.

Be this as it may, it is probable that the

Romans, along with their other habits and fashions, imported the various games which they played with the *follis* or with other kinds of ball, into England. One of these balls, used by the Romans, and by them derived from the Greeks, was the *harpastum*, the game played with which was that the players of one side should try to carry the ball over a line defended by the other side, a pastime which bears no small resemblance to the game of " hurling," which we shall describe later. But whether football was really introduced into Britain by the Romans, or whether it be an indigenous product of the country, yet, with the exception of the one doubtful reference to an anonymous manuscript to which allusion has formerly been made, we do not find any mention of the game in the annals of our Anglo-Saxon progenitors; and it is not until the 13th century that we find genuine historical authority on the subject.

CHAPTER II.

History of Football before the Puritan Era.

THE first mention of the game of football in English history is made by Fitz-Stephen, who, writing in the 13th century, says, "Annually upon Shrove Tuesday they (the London school-boys) go into the fields immediately after dinner and play at the celebrated game of ball (*ludum pilæ celebrem*)." But it is only fair to add, that the learned Strutt himself never felt certain that the reference here was to football. He tells us, in his commentary upon the passage, that Stowe, in his explanation of the words, has added, "without the least sanction from the Latin," the word bastion, "meaning a bat or cudgel," being of opinion that the game signified was something of the nature of goff (golf) or bandy-ball (*sc.*, hockey). If Stowe was guilty of this bold gloss, and there is no question that he was, then it is clear that the game of the London school-boys is as likely to have been football as anything else, although Strutt is of the contrary opinion. For Strutt's view is based upon the ground that football, as a pastime, " does not seem to be a very proper game for children." On the other hand, there are strong reasons for believing that this game may have been football, for in the first place there is good historical evidence to the effect that Shrove-Tuesday was a regular day upon which the London apprentices and those of other great cities, such as Chester, and the Scotch peasants, regularly indulged in the game of football. This evidence will be set forth immediately. But it is also a matter to be noted, that London is one of the places where football seems never to have died out, while the London schools, notably Westminster and the Charterhouse, were the places in which one species of the game of football was kept alive in a period of great athletic depression, to emerge, at the time of the recent athletic revival, in the form of the Association game.

That this game flourished in the succeeding century is manifest from the fact that Edward III., in A.D. 1349, found it necessary to forbid it by law. This warlike monarch, who was not quite of the same opinion as a man of at least equally military mind, the Duke of Wellington, sent a

formal letter of complaint to the sheriffs of the
City of London, that "the skill in shooting with
arrows was almost totally laid aside for the
purpose of various useless and unlawful games,"
and they were thenceforth enjoined to prohibit all
such "idle practices" as far as their jurisdiction
extended.

Football, however, seemed to have sufficient
vitality to outlast the pressure of a statute which,
like some of those at present directed against
gambling and betting, seems to have been more
honoured in the breach than in the observance,
for we find that in 1389 another Act was passed
by Richard II. (12 Ric. ii., cap. 6) for the purpose
of encouraging shooting, at the expense of other
sports.   This Act expressly forbade throughout
the kingdom "all playinge at Tennis, Footballe,
and other games called corts, dice, casting of the
stone, kailes (a kind of skittles), and other such
importune games."   How great must have been
the moral effect of the statute we see from the fact
that it had to be re-enacted by Henry IV. in
1401, and again by Henry VIII. considerably
more than a hundred years later ; while the last-
named monarch also passed an enactment render-
ing it a penal offence for any person whatever to
attempt to make gain by keeping a house or ground

for sporting purposes of any kind—an enactment which some of the present managers of "gate-money" meetings for amateurs would be doubtless sorry to see replaced upon the Statute Book. Another clause of the same Act made it a penal offence for an artificer to play at any of the games mentioned above, save at Christmastide. In Scotland also similar measures were pursued for the purpose of separating those canny sportsmen from their well-loved games of golf and football; for in 1458, James III. of Scotland decreed that displays of weapons were to be held four times a year, and that "footballe and golfe be utterly put down." Two other pieces of evidence show how constant and how vain was the effort made by our sovereigns to suppress a national sport. Twice in the reign of Elizabeth was proclamation made that "no foteballe play be used or suffered within the City of London and the liberties thereof, upon pain of imprisonment," and twice were entries of the proclamations having been made entered in the books of the Corporation of London, upon Nov. 27th, 1572, and Nov. 7th, 1581, where they can be seen to this day. But in spite of prohibition and threat of fine and imprisonment, the London apprentices and the country labourers were determined to enjoy their football; and the game was probably never so flourishing or so prosperous as it was throughout the sixteenth century.

And now, it may be asked, What manner of game was this football, which delighted our forefathers so hugely that they persisted in indulging in it although under ban of the law? Strange to say, there was not the chaos of conflicting rules which were found in use when the game was brought into prominence again a few decades ago. The original game appears to have been of the simplest description. Given two boundaries or goals, a ball of any make so long as it were strong enough to prevent its being torn in pieces, and the opposing sides were allowed to get the ball on and make it touch the adversaries' goal in any manner whatever they pleased, whether by kicking, hurling, shoving, or running, or by stealth. Sometimes we hear of goals a mile or more apart; often the arena of play was a street or a high road, sometimes a whole town; and the attacking party with the ball would try and sneak round by bye-streets in order to escape notice, and plant the ball unawares through the window or against the post which was fixed as the goal. The game, in short, when played in a confined space, was none other than a rough form of the present Rugby Union football, without the rules and prohibitions which have now reduced to order and civilized that game. But it must have been a rough game, that of which the yokels and 'prentices of merry England were so fond; and of broken pates and aching shins there must have been not a few. But let us hear what the writers of the age had to say about it. But before we proceed to give a few extracts of their views, we must premise that football was always looked upon as a vulgar game, a game for clod-hoppers, Irish kernes, and 'prentice lads, which a gentleman of quality should shun, lest perchance his eye be blackened or his skin be raised in lumps by a wight of low degree. Hence we can only expect the writers of gentle birth of the age of Elizabeth and James I., and indeed of all the later ages up to the present generation, to look upon so rough a game as unfitting for a man of refinement. But a game does not need to be defended now because it brings men of different rank to meet on equal terms with no favour; and ardent footballers might indeed be still able to adhere to their game although it had been deemed vulgar by James I. and by Sir Thomas Elyot. Nor is there anything in the contempt of these dignitaries which will depress the spirits or hurt the sensitive pride of the football player especially; for he will find upon study that football was not the only game condemned by the aristocratic classes. On the contrary, almost all athletic exercises which did not immediately and obviously conduce to knightly skill, were held in equally low esteem; and the game of cricket itself was equally lightly regarded. In fact, it is not too much to say, that it was not until the present century was well advanced that men of gentle birth and education gave up putting away boyish sports when they reached man's estate. But of this we shall speak later.

The earliest writers who discuss football critically, are of the Elizabethan era. We have indeed been informed by a learned antiquary to whom we are largely indebted for the materials of this work, that many years before this there flourished in the City of London a "Guild of Football Players;" but as our friend has lost his reference to this, the first Football Club in existence, and as we have been unable, with much searching, to recover the clue, we are unable to present to our readers any report of exciting matches between the representatives of the various wards or between the opposing teams of the cities of London and Westminster. But of the fact that such an organization existed we feel little or no doubt, and only regret we cannot give more accurate information on the subject. We can only close our notice of the subject by transcribing the comment of the gentle scholar to whom we are indebted for the suggestion, that "probably the players, recognising the danger of the game to soul and body, thought it necessary to combine to employ a special chirurgeon, and a special chaplain of their own," from which it will be seen that our friend is more fond of antiquities than he is of football.

The first Elizabethan critic of football whose words deserve quotation, is Sir Thomas Elyot, the author of "The Boke called the Governour," a species of educational manual for the young noblemen and gentlemen of the age. Writing, in 1583, of the sports which should be indulged in by those of gentle birth, he expounds views which, seen through the glass of the opinions of the nineteenth century, appear strange. Archery he praises above tennis, because in tennis a player is compelled to play as hard as his opponent, and cannot, so to speak, make his own pace; so that "if he (the opponent) stryke the balle hard, the othere that intendeth to receyve him is then constrained to use semblable violence if he wyll to retourne the balle." And "boulynge" (bowls), "claishe," and "pinnes" (skittles), and "koyting" (quoits), are also spoken of with disfavour as being too furious; and the writer then goes on (we quote *verbatim*, leaving more learned critics to explain the worthy knight's grammar): "Verilie as for two the laste" (*i.e.*, pinnes and koyting) be to be utterly abjected of all noble men, in like wise foote balle wherein is nothing but beastlie furie and exstreme violence, whereof procedeth hurte and consequently rancour and malice do remaine with them that be wounded, wherfore it is to be put in perpetuall silence." Perhaps this view would have been coincided with by a certain bridegroom whom we read elsewhere to have attended the revels held at Kenilworth in honour of Queen Elizabeth in 1575, for the gentleman in question, we gather from a letter of the gallant Captain Laneham, to have been "lame of a legge, that in his youth was broeken at footeballe;" but modern footballers would hardly agree with Sir Thomas or with the learned and pious Puritan writer, Stubbs, who, in our quotations, "follows on the same side." Stubbs, in his "Anatomie of Abuses" in the realm of England in 1583, not only objected to football for itself, but also for that it was generally played, both in town and village, on Sunday; and one of his reasons for believing that the day of doom, as foretold in

Scriptural revelation, was at hand was, that "football playing and other develishe pastimes" were played on Sunday. "Lord," he prays, "remove these exercises from the Sabaoth." What follows is curious: in answer to a question as to whether football-playing is a profanation of the Sabbath, he says, "Any exercise which withdraweth us from godlinesse, either upon the Sabaoth or any other day, is wicked and to be forbiden. Now who is so grossly blinde that seeth not that these aforesaid exercises not only withdraw us from godlinesse and virtue, but also haile and allure us to wickednesse and sin? for as concerning football playing, I protest unto you it may rather be called a friendlie kind of fight than a play or recreation —a bloody and murthering practise than a felowly sporte or pastime. For dooth not everyone lye in waight for his adversarie, seeking to overthrow him and picke him on his nose, though it be on hard stones, in ditch or dale, in valley or hill, or what place soever it be he careth not, so he have him downe. And he that can serve the most of this fashion, he is counted the only felow and who but he." We may remark incidentally that it is at least satisfactory to know that the footballers of the time of Elizabeth appreciated the advantages of a good "tackler." But to resume with

Stubbs his opinions. "So that by this means sometimes their necks are broken, sometimes their backs, sometimes their legs, sometimes their armes, sometimes one part thrust out of joint, sometimes another; sometimes their noses gush out with blood, sometimes their eyes start out, and sometimes hurte in one place sometimes in another. But whosoever scapeth away the best goeth not scot free but is either forewounded, craised or bruised so as he dyeth of it or else scapeth very hardlie, and no mervaile, for they have the sleights to meet one betwixt two, to dash him against the hart with their elbowes, to butt him under the short ribs with the griped fists and with their knees to catch him on the hip and pick him on his neck, with a hundred such murthering devices. And hereof groweth envy, rancour, and malice, and sometimes brawling murther, homicide, and great effusion of blood, as experience daily teacheth. Is this murthering play now an exercise for the Sabaoth day?"

So much for the opinion of the pious Stubbs, who, it must be recollected, was a Puritan, and one of the party who afterwards almost succeeded in entirely putting down football during the supremacy of their opinions. Perhaps it will be as well to finish the hostile criticism with the opinion of

King James I. of England, who, in his Basilicon
Doron, a manual of education written for his son,
after speaking in praise of various other sports,
saith, " but from this count I debar all rough and
violent exercise, as the foot-ball meeter for laming
than making able the users thereof." Still James
I., taking him for all in all, was something of an
old woman, and can hardly have been expected to
look with favour upon a " charge " or a " scrimmage." Added to this, we have something more
than a suspicion that his Royal Highness, while
posing as an original writer on education, was
drawing a great many of his views from Sir Thomas
Elyot; for the Basilicon Doron bears a most
suspicious resemblance in many places to the work
of the earlier writer.

Perhaps the best description we have of the
game at this period comes from Carew's "Survey
of Cornwall," published in 1602. Carew gives a
long account of the game of " hurling," which was
another form of the football we have described
above, with the addition that the players were
allowed, if they liked, to carry sticks and hit the
ball towards the goal, besides hurling, kicking,
hitting, or running with it. We thus see, as would
naturally be expected, that hockey and football
started as the same sport but gradually " differenti-

ated" into separate games, according to the true Darwinian law of progress. Hurling is described as a match between two large parties of men, in which each side strives to get the ball as best it can up to the adversaries' goal. Carew, who is a more genial critic than Elyot, Stubbs, or King James I., describes hurling with much carefulness and acuteness of observation. "For hurling to goales there are 15, 20, or 30 players, more or less, chosen out on each side, who strip themselves to their slightest apparel and then join hands in ranke one against another; out of these ranks they matche themselves by payres, one embracing another, and so passe away, every of which couple are especially to watch one another during the play." What football player knows not the phrase, "Mark your men?" "After this, they pitch two bushes in the ground, some eight or ten feet asunder, and directly against them, ten or twelve score places off, other twain in like distance, which they term goales, where some indifferent person throweth up a balle, the which whosoever can catch and carry through the adversaries' goals hath won the game." The hurlers also, we learn, were not allowed to *but* or *handfast* (charge or collar) under the girdle, or to "deale a foreballe" *i.e.*, to pass forward to one nearer the goal than the

player, in which passage we have the only explicit
reference to "offside" play which is to be found in
the early annals of the game. Besides the game
in a field of play, there was also, we learn from
Carew, a game played over country. "Two
three or more parishes agree to hurl against two
or three other parishes." In this game the goals
were usually houses, or else villages, three or four
miles asunder, and "that company which can
catch or carry it by force or slight to the place
assigned, gaineth the victory. Such as see where
the ball is played give notice, by crying, 'Ware east,'
'Ware west,' as the same is carried. The hurlers
take their way over hilles, dales, hedges, ditches,
yea, and thorow bushes, briars, mires, plashes and
rivers whatsoever, so as you shall sometimes see
twenty or thirty lie tugging together in the water,
scrambling and scratching for the ball." This
description of what may be described as a "maul
in pond" is certainly interesting, and the whole
description of the game lucid. The criticism of
the game is also eminently sensible. "The play
is verily both rude and rough, yet such as is not
destitute of policies in some sort resembling the
feats of war; for you shall have companies laid
out before, on the one side to encounter them that
come with the ball, and of the other party to

succour them in manner of a fore-ward." (Thus
we see that the term "forward" in football is no
ill-chosen one, the "fore-wards" or "fore-guards"
being those who bear the first attack, and protect
the rear-guards, who are manœuvring behind.)
Carew goes on, "The ball in this play may be
compared to an infernal spirit, for whosoever catch-
eth it fareth straightways like a madman strug-
gling and fighting with those that go about to hold
him : no sooner is the ball gone from him than he
resigneth this fury to the next receiver, and himself becometh peaceable as before." (Perhaps, we
may here remark, the man who lost the ball became peaceable because he was by that time well
" blown." We have observed the same ourselves
in the present age.) Carew ends up with some
very thoughtful criticism of the game, " I cannot
well resolve," he says, "whether I should the more
commend this game for its manhood and exercise,
or condemn it for the boisterousness and harm
which it begetteth ; for as on the one side it makes
their bodies strong, hard, and nimble, and puts a
courage into their hearts to meet an enemy in the
face, so on the other part it is accompanied by
many dangers, some of which do ever fall to the
players' share, for the proof whereof when the
hurling is ended, you shall see them retiring home

as from a pitched battle, with bloody pates, bones broken and out of joint, and such bruises as serve to shorten their days; yet all is good play, and never attorney or coroner troubled for the matter."

Perhaps one more extract will be sufficient to show that *circiter* A.D. 1600, football was considered one of the national sports of England, just as it is to-day. Here is a list of British games in the year 1600. Quoth one bold swain to another his rival (in verse) :—

> " Man, I dare challenge thee to throw the sledge,
>   To jumpe, or leape over a ditch or hedge ;
>   To wrastle, play at stooleballe, or to runne,
>   To pitch the barre, or to shoote off a gunne ;
>   To play at loggets, nine-holes, or ten pinnes,
>   *To trie it out at football by the shinnes,*
>   To dance the morris, play at barley breake,
>   At all esploytes a man can think or speake.
>   At shove-groate, venter-poynte, or crosse and pile,
>   At beshrow him that's the last at yonder stile. "

Perhaps, gentle reader, we may have more to say anon about the ancient sports of the age of Shakspeare, but at present we must needs jog on. Let not our readers think, however, that the Bard of Avon never heard of football. Let them look to the " Comedy of Errors," Act ii. Scene 6,—

> " Am I so round with you as you with me,
>   That like a football you do spurn me thus ?

> You spurn me hence and he will spurn me hither,
> If I last in this service, you must case me in leather."

Lear too, and Kent, knew something about "hacking" and "tripping." Listen to this, "Lear," Act i. Scene 4.

Lear.   Do you bandy looks with me, you rascal?
Steward.   I'll not be strucken, my lord.
Kent.   Nor tripped neither, you base football-player (tripping up his heels).
Lear.   I thank thee, fellow.

Lear, you see, breaks out into an exclamation of praise, when he sees a neat "trip" brought off by Kent.

There are still some ancient customs in relation to the game of football, which belong to no particular age, as many of them endured through many ages, but which may well be set out here lest they should pass out of mind. The following is from MS. Harl. 2150, fol. 235 :—"It hath been the custom, time out of mind, for the shoemakers yearly on Shrove Tuesday to deliver to the drapers, in the presence of the Mayor of Chester, at the cross on the Rodehee, one ball of leather called a foote ball, of the value of three shillings and fourpence and above, to play at from thence to the Common Hall of the said city ; which practice was productive of much inconvenience ; and this year

(1540), by consent of the parties concerned, the ball was changed into six glayves of silver of the like value, as a reward for the best runner that day upon the aforesaid Rodehee."

At the parish of Scone, in Perthshire, a similar game appears to have been played every Shrove Tuesday, between the bachelors and the married men, from two o'clock until sunset. The game was initiated by the throwing up of the ball in the neighbourhood of the market cross at Scone, and the account of it may well be given in the words of the author of " The Statistical Account of Scotland," as quoted by Hone in his Year-Book of 1838. The game was this : " He who at any time got the ball into his hands ran with it till overtaken by one of the opposite party, and then, if he could shake himself loose from those of the opposite party who seized him, he ran on; if not, he threw the ball from him, unless it was wrested from him by the other party, *but no person was allowed to kick it.* The object of the married men was to hang it, that is, to put it three times into a small hole in the moor, which was the ' dool,' or limit, on the one hand ; that of the bachelors was to drown it, or dip it three times in a deep place in the river, the limit on the other ; the party who could effect either of these objects won the game; if neither won, the ball was cut into equal parts at sunset.   In the course of the play there was usually some violence between the parties; but it is a proverb in this part of the country, that 'All is fair at the ball at Scone.'" This annual game is supposed to have been established in commemoration of the victory of a parishioner of Scone over an Italian braggadocio of chivalrous times; and every man in the parish was compelled to play.   Thus, in this Perthshire game we seem to find the rough and rude instance of the original game in Scotland, and the first instance of compulsory football.   It should further be remarked, that the same antiquary gives an account of an annual Shrove Tuesday football match between the married women of Inverness and the spinsters of the same parish, which, according to him, invariably resulted in the triumph of the married women.   It appears, therefore, that the female elevens which occasionally appear in North Country football fields, are not without a respectable historical precedent for their acts.   Still, it is pardonable to say that the game is not exactly suitable to their physical constitution ; and even the sturdy lass of Inverness must have been somewhat out of place in the game which Waller decribes with reasonable accuracy in the following lines :—

> " As when a sort of lustie shepherd's boy
>   Their force at football ; care of victory
>   Makes them salute so rudely breast to breast,
>   That their encounter seems too rough for jest."

A game of similar character to "the ball at Scone" appears also to have been played yearly at Kingston-on-Thames on Shrove Tuesday, which, as we shall see later, continued an annual fixture until far into the present century.

Sunday was a great day for all sports and pastimes throughout the Tudor times ; and it was long indeed before the Puritan reaction caused them to be entirely stopped on that day. There is an amusing extract from Thomas Cartwright's Admonition to Parliament, which gives some material for the formation of an idea of the manner in which our forefathers spent the Sunday. It should be mentioned that the learned writer originally wrote with the object of showing that an established form of prayer was unsuitable for church service. "Among his arguments," says the easily-satisfied historian, "is the following :—'He,' meaning the minister, 'posteth it over as fast as he can galloppe; for eyther he hath two places to serve, or else there are some games to be playde in the afternoon, as lying for the whetstone, heathenishe dauncing for the ring, a beare or a bulle to be baited, or else a jackanapes to ride on horsebacke, or an interlude to be playde. And, if no place else can be gotten, this interlude must be plaide in the church.'" And, in order that a clear idea of the details of Sunday life may be obtained, the antiquary adds an extract from "The Pope's Kingdom" (1570), translated from the Latin of T. Neorgeorgus by Barnaby Googe :—

" Now when the dinner our is done, and that they well
        have fed,
    To play they go; to casting of the stone, to runne or
        shoote ;
    To tosse the light and windy ball aloft with hand or foote ;
    Some others trie their skille in gonnes ; some wrastel all
        the day ;
    And some to schooles of fence do goe, to gaze upon the
        play ;
    Another sort there is that does not love abroad to roame,
    But for to pass their time at cardes, or tables, still at home."

Writings of this kind were abundant in the time of Elizabeth, and eventually became so influential as to cause that most prudent of stateswomen to issue a general proclamation enjoining a more strict observance of the Sabbath. It would be most erroneous, however, to trace in this proclamation any characteristic quality of Elizabeth other than natural prudence, for there have been few English monarchs, male or female, to whom the Puritan tenets were more distasteful at heart than they were to the peerless but somewhat out-spoken virgin queen.   James I., for whom Strutt has a great admiration, repeated this declaration in general; but he, as a timid man, averse to muscular exercise, and an indifferent sportsman, had a rooted objection to football, which, as we have stated before, was not wonderful.

Enough has now been written to prove that the game of football is, in name at least, of extreme antiquity, and to give a general idea of its characteristics in early times.   But it may not be amiss to examine these latter in more detail.   It is to be noted in the first place that there appear in early days to have been hardly any rules; but it is nevertheless possible to discover certain general characteristics.   The main principle of the game appears to have been, that a ball should be driven from one place to another; but as to the means appropriate to its conveyance, there would seem to have been a great difference.   The men of Perthshire never, by any chance, kicked the ball; the Southerners kicked, carried, and struck it with their hands or with sticks.

But for any trace of what is now known as the Association game, in which almost the only method of propulsion of the ball allowed is by kicking with the feet, we look in vain in ancient times.   It seems probable that such a game originated in schools, and was confined to them, until brought before the public as a pastime for men by school-boys from the great public foundations, who wished to continue their games after they had left school for the world.   The real and substantial difference between the two games as at present played is, that in the Association game no collaring, and therefore no running with the ball, is allowed ; so that it may be not unsafe to conjecture that the dribbling game was invented, or rather grew, in schools where young boys were not allowed to tear each others' clothes and break each others' bones in the intervals of school hours.   But of the Association game we shall have more to say anon.

We think we have said enough of the history of the game of football in the days preceding the Great Revolution and the Puritan supremacy. This was a period in which the star of athleticism waned to an exceeding paleness; and there is no question that those who appreciate the benefits of innocent enjoyment in exercise of the body, owe a deep debt of enmity to the Roundheads.   With their politics, their religion, their love of independence, and with many other points good and bad in their character, we have no concern in the present work.

The death of Charles on the scaffold, the history of the Long Parliament, Cromwell with his spot of blood upon his collar, the steeple-crowned hats, and the sad-coloured cloaks touch us not at all. But the influence which the Puritans exercised in determining the pastimes of the nation is a serious matter. From an athletic point of view, the Puritan creed is this—" Be always morose, always ponderous, absorbed in continual thought and everlasting sermonizing concerning your latter end. Now, if you play football or cricket, or indulge in any English pastimes, you will unquestionably forget your latter end, and will develop such a healthy energy as will be fatal to despondent bitterness of spirit, which makes the true Puritan." The result was simple. Exercise was a waste of time, innocent pleasure an unwarrantable pampering of the flesh, an unholy coaxing of the old Adam. Now we all know the result of insufficient exercise to be derangement of the liver, the spleen, and all organs and functions of the body. Upon this follows loss of temper, which passes from the condition of casual irritability to that of unre-lenting and constitutional rancour. Thus men of dispositions naturally bitter and gloomy, not only took steps to develop their naturally ungracious tendencies, but also sought to run the rest of the nation into the same mould. They did their endeavour to convert merry England,—for we were once, in very truth, the merriest of nations,— into a melancholy country; and it may well be believed that the Restoration was due as much to weariness of the Puritan discipline in matters of daily life and amusement, as to any strong political feeling. The rule of politics which the Puritans seem to have forgotten, is the practical one, that the first principle of good government is to keep the people who are governed in a good humour. The natural result of a system which inculcated bitterness of thought, fostered ill-humour, and encouraged conceit, was, that it should perish at the hands of the bitterness, the ill-humour, and conceit which it had itself engendered.

CHAPTER III.

*History of Football from the Puritan Era until
the Present Century.*

AFTER the downfall of the Puritan Government and of the supremacy of Puritan
opinions, as every student of history
well knows, the Maypoles were set up again in
the country, and simple folk resumed their dancing and the like rustic sports. But it is rather the
fashion of concise historians to represent changes
of this kind as more rapid than they are in actual
fact; and it is probably nearer the truth to say that
the Puritan habits and feelings which came over
England in the earlier part of the 17th century
have never really lost their hold of the nation, and
are even in this day dying hard. Certain it is, at
any rate, if any certainty can be gathered from
the literature which is, as it were, the crystallized
thought of an age, that until the present generation athletic sports have never so much formed a
part of the life of the English people as they did

D

before the Puritan epoch. The direction of a straw is sufficient to show which way the wind is blowing; and the apparently insignificant fact that references to football and other early English games are rare in the literature of the eighteenth century, is almost sufficient in itself to prove the decrease in the popularity of the game. Some old towns and districts clung to the ancient and simple form of the game, and cling to it still up to the present day; but it will not be too much to say, that from the date of the Restoration until the time of the great athletic revival in the last thirty or forty years, the popularity of the ancient game of football was steadily declining, though never in any danger of complete extinction. Let us give the generation who abandoned their ardour for football their due, and say that they became more serious, more earnest, and less brutal in their sports. The fact, however, of the decline in the popularity of the game remains the same, and with the chronicling of that fact we must remain content. So early as 1675 we learn from a satire that the apprentices of London were no longer content with a game of football on Shrove Tuesday or any such holiday, but preferred the by no means modern amusement of a political demonstration. Says the anonymous satirist of the 'prentices,—

> "They're mounted high, contemn the humble play
>   Of rap or foot-ball on a holiday
>   In Fines-bury-fieldes.   No ; 'tis their brave intent
>   Wisely t' advise the king and parliament."

Still the city youths were not always indulging in demonstrations about this time, and a number of games of football were played about the metropolis after the Restoration. In 1665 Pepys records in his diary that on January the 2nd, the streets were full of footballs, it being a great frost. Probably the footballers of that time did not play football for choice when the ground was frozen ; but a long frost meant a long holiday and cessation from business in those good old times, and the 'prentices therefore got an opportunity of playing the game which they would not have had in open weather. We hear too of a match played in 1681 between the servants of King Charles II. and those of the Duke of Albemarle, which the king witnessed himself and was much delighted at. A few years later, there was enough football in London to attract the notice of a French visitor, M. Misson, who published his views of England at the end of the 17th century in a book brought out at Paris in the year 1698, and entitled " Mémoires et Observations Faites par un Voyageur." We need hardly wonder that the

Frenchman in his description of the game should be unable to appreciate its exact significance. Simple as the game undoubtedly was in these days, there was probably a little more "science" in it than the visitor to our shores could comprehend. These are his words : " En hiver le Football est un exercice utile et charmant. C'est un balon de cuir, gros comme la tête et rempli de vent : cela se balotte avec le pied dans les rues par celui qui le peut attraper : il n'y a point d'autre science." From this very short allusion in a long work some very interesting pieces of information are to be derived. First, it appears that at this time the football had definitely assumed somewhat of its present shape : it was a leather ball, full of wind, as large as a man's head. Next we find that football was definitely regarded by a foreigner as a regular winter sport in England, and that it was still played as an ordinary matter of course in the streets or public places. A third inference may possibly be drawn from the passage. M. Misson speaks of no running or collaring, but merely of kicking with the feet. Here at last might the dribbler think that we find a definite allusion to the original dribbling or Association game. After consideration, however, we think that a different explanation of the passage is probably to be given.

From the description we have quoted, it seems probable that the writer had not seen a genuine football match, but merely boys or men kicking a football about the streets for amusement,—in modern phraseology "having a punt-about." Whichever interpretation of the passage, however, be taken, it seems not improbable that it was from the custom of punting a ball about in a confined space for the sake of obtaining warmth and exercise upon a cold day, without any running with the ball or rough horse-play, that the proficiency in dribbling and kicking was first obtained and the capacities of the dribbling game for affording a genuine sport full of skill and excitement first discovered. On the whole, however, there is little doubt that the Association game must be regarded as the product of the great public schools of the kingdom, and not so much the national sport of the lower classes.

The Spectator, which in other respects forms a mine of wealth for procuring information as to the customs and opinions of England in the beginning of the 18th century, is, unfortunately for our purpose, almost entirely silent as to the game of football. There is, however, an illusion in No. 161 (Sept. 4th, 1711). A supposed country correspondent, a dweller in the neighbourhood of the estate of Sir Roger de Coverley, writes to *The Spectator* in town an account of a country wake. First the writer finds "a ring of cudgel-players, who were breaking one anothers' heads in order to make some impression upon their mistresses' hearts." "I observed," he goes on, "a lusty young fellow who had the misfortune of a broken pate, but what considerably added to the anguish of the wound, was his overhearing an old man who shook his head and said, 'that he questioned now if black Kate would marry him these three years.' I was diverted from a further observation of these combatants by a football match which was on the other side of the green, where Tom Short behaved himself so well that most people seemed to agree it was impossible that he should remain a bachelor until the next wake. Having played many a match myself, I could have looked longer on the sport, had I not observed a country girl." . . . And so, forsooth, the *Spectator's* country correspondent gives up the further contemplation and probably the further description of a manly game, in order that he may gaze at a country wench, to the great detriment and loss of knowledge of the football student of the present day. O woman, woman, how many omissions are to be laid to thy charge through the vanity and curiosity of man.

when he gazeth upon thee!   At any rate, however,
we gather from the passage that in the 18th
century the country people played at football in
holiday time on the village green, that country
gentlemen joined in the matches, and that the
most skilful players gained the favour and en-
couragement of the fair sex, and were not destined
to remain bachelors for ever.   Verily, ye gentlemen
of Blackheath, times are changed, but not manners.

In writing however of the 18th century, the
learned Strutt is the safest guide, for his com-
pilations and researches into matters of ancient
sport take us up to the end of the 18th century.
From Strutt we learn how the game was gradually
being abandoned throughout the country about the
year 1800.   " Of late years," he says, " it seems to
have fallen into disrepute, and is but little practised."   We see, however, from his amusing description which follows, that by his time it had become
a field sport, and was played upon a regular football
field, and doubtless with touch-lines and goal-lines.
Unfortunately he makes no mention of the number
of players who are usually engaged in the contest,
and gives us little or no hint of any rule, or any
explanation of what was considered scientific play.
" When," he says, "a match at football is made,
two parties, each containing an equal number of

competitors, take the field, and stand between two goals, placed at the distance of eighty or an hundred yards the one from the other. The goal is usually made with two sticks driven into the ground about two or three feet apart. The ball, which is commonly made of a blown bladder and cased with leather, is delivered in the midst of the ground, and the object of each party is to drive it through the goal of the other, which being achieved the game is won. . . . When the exercise becomes exceeding violent, the players kick each others' shins without the least ceremony, and some of them are overthrown at the hazard of their limbs." He garnishes his simple account with some elegant extracts from Barclay and Waller, such as—

> " The sturdie plowman, lustie, strong, and bold,
> Overcometh the winter by driving the foote-ball,
> Forgetting labour and many a grievous fall."

and again—

> " And now in winter when men kill the fat swine,
> They get the bladder and blow it great and thin,
> With many beans and peason put therein :
> It rattleth, soundeth, and shineth clere and fayre ;
> While it is thrown and caste up in the ayre,
> Each one contendeth and hath a great delite
> With foot and with hand, the bladder for to smite ;
> If it fall to ground they lift it up again,
> And this waye to labour they count it no payne."

From the time of Strutt, whose book was published in 1801, until the great revival of the game, about fifty years later, there is little to chronicle in the history of the game, which was played at almost all the great schools; but, as regards the rest of the world, only popular in certain localities where great matches were played by those who adhered to ancient customs. In fact, we find from the mention made of the game by Hone, the author of the " Every Day Book and Year Book," that football for men was looked upon as more or less of a relic of antiquity in England. There was the celebrated match at Kingston on Shrove Tuesday, at Corfe Castle in Dorsetshire, the equally celebrated antiquity at Derby, at which city, as reported by Glover, its learned historian, a match had been played every year on Shrove Tuesday since A.D. 217, when a troop of British warriors thrust some Roman troops out of the gates. But what Hone states of England seems never to have applied to Scotland and a few northern counties of England, where the game has enjoyed an uninterrupted popularity among the inhabitants of the country. But perhaps a better idea can be obtained by giving some of Hone's extracts. On page 152 of his " Year Book " (1852), he quotes, from Hutchinson's " History of Cumberland," an account of the football match at Bromfield, on Shrove Tuesday. The scholars of the free school in that place were allowed by custom to "bar out" the master for three days; after a mock fight with popguns and harmless missiles, a truce was solemnly concluded, one of the terms of which was, that a football match should be permitted, as well as some cock-fighting. "After the cock-fighting was ended," says the account, "the football was thrown down in the churchyard, and the point then contended was, which party should carry it to the house of his respective captain—to Dundraw perhaps or West Newton, a distance of two or three miles. The details of these matches were the general topics of conversation among the villagers, and were dwelt on with hardly less satisfaction than their ancestors enjoyed in relating their feats in the border wars." A quotation of an indigenous song is also given, which runs as follows :—

" At Scales, great Tom Barmes got the ba' in his hand,
  And t'wives all ran out and shouted and banned ;
  Tom Cowan then pulched and flang him 'mang t' whins,
  And he bleddered ' Od-white-te ' tou's broken my shins."

An account of a similar game at Kingston in the year 1815, is given in the " Every Day Book," vol. i., p. 245.

A correspondent writes to the Editor to say that
when travelling by the Hampton Court coach to
Kingston on Shrove Tuesday, he was told that it
was " Football Day," and "was not a little amused
to see, upon entering Teddington, all the inhabitants
securing the glass of their front windows by placing
hurdles before them, and some by nailing laths.
At Twickenham, Bushy, and Hampton Wick they
were all engaged in the same way. Having to
stop a few hours at Kingston, I had an opportunity
of seeing the whole custom. . . . At about 12
o'clock the ball is turned loose, and those who can
kick it. I observed some persons of respectability
following the ball : the game lasts about four hours,
when the parties retire to the public-houses." . . .
The writer goes on to say that the corporation of
Kingston tried to put a stop to the practice; but
the judges confirmed the right to the game.

Another correspondent, whose letter is published
on page 374 of vol. ii. of the same book, describes
how at that time (viz. 1827), a game of football
was played every Sunday afternoon by Irishmen,
upon an open space at Islington. The game
commenced at three, and lasted until dusk, men
of one county, as a rule, playing against men of
another. The same writer goes on to say that when
he was a boy he was accustomed to play football

on a Sunday morning in the "church-piece" before church-time, in a village in the West of England; but from the tone of the letter it appears very evident that the writer looked upon football at that day as a game more of the past than of the present.

In Scotland, however, football in this age was still a national pastime, and extensively patronized by the upper classes. In 1815 we read of a great football match being played at Carterhaugh in Ettrick Forest, between the Ettrick men and the men of Yarrow; the one party backed by the Earl of Home, and the other by Sir Walter Scott, then Sheriff of the forest. The latter wrote a couple of songs in honour of the occasion, from one of which we quote a verse,—

" Then strip, lads, and to it, though sharp be the weather ;
    And if by mischance you should happen to fall,
  There are worse things in life than a tumble on heather,
    And life is itself but a game of football."

It is perhaps scarcely necessary to quote the lines from the " Lay of the Last Minstrel," of the same poet, when, in the truce between the English and Scottish armies, sports were indulged in :—

" Some drive the jolly bowl about ;
    With dice and draughts some chase the day ;
  And some, with many a merry shout,
    In riot, revelry, and rout,
  Pursue the football play."

But independently of these extracts, there are many allusions through Scott's works which testify to the acknowledged popularity of football in Scotland in the lifetime of the great novelist.

Perhaps we cannot do better than conclude our account of the football of the past before the days of the Rugby Union and Association rules by referring to the ancient game which is still played at Derby on Shrove Tuesday at the present, though perhaps played with less zest since the lusty youths of the city have had plenty of opportunities of enjoying the game to the top of their bent on other occasions, and since too we live in an age which has more respect for the privileges and feelings of peaceable householders than its predecessors. At Derby there has been from time immemorial a match at football on Shrove Tuesday, between the rival parishes of All Saints and St. Peter. The game is started in the market-place, and the St. Peter's goal is a gate some miles away, while the wheel of a water-mill, distant about as far, is the goal of the All Saints' division; and the game is over when the ball has been taken to either goal. Rules of the game there are none; and all that is needed is for one party, by force or by stratagem, to get the ball up to the adversary's goal; to effect which object, *détours* are made round streets and alleys, and the river often crossed by swimming with the ball. Here indeed is a survival of one of the ancient sports of merrie England, where blows are given and taken in good humour, and "all is good play, and never attorney or coroner troubled for the matter." Nor is Derby by any means the only place where such a game is still played. In the Midlands, the North, the South, and the West it survives in holes and corners of old England; and although we who have learnt the game of football in other days may prefer a good match with picked sides on the regulation field of play and under organized rules, yet we should regard with veneration the more simple sport from which has been derived the more elaborate game which it was our delight to play in youth, and which it may be our delight to watch in old age. We must reserve for another chapter the important task of showing how, issuing from its home in the public schools, where it had for generations found a welcome shelter, the game of football has developed once more in our days into a national sport.

CHAPTER IV.

History of Football in the Public Schools.

IT is vastly to the credit of cricket and of football that they should have survived the Puritan deluge and the decay of the athletic spirit at the end of the last century, and not have been laid in limbo together with stoolball, cambuc, and other games wherein the hearts of our forefathers rejoiced. The survival indicates an exceeding fitness. Still the storm of Puritanical hatred had been enough to kill even hardier plants than these, unless there had been some quiet haunts in which they existed unnoticed and unmolested. As to the pastimes of the 'prentice boys they perished; but in the quiet privacy of the country and in the almost monastic seclusion of some of our ancient public schools they continued to exist.

For some reason or other, the foundation of Laurence Sheriff, at Rugby, was the locality in which, what we now call the Rugby game, but which, for reasons above mentioned, appears in reality to have been the pristine form of the game, was preserved. Now, since of every effect there is a cause, and since of this particular effect history supplies no cause that we are aware of, it becomes necessary to have recourse to conjecture; and since conjecture, to be probable, must proceed upon some sound basis, it seems to follow, that in order to discover why the game, distinguished by an absence of rules, survived in Rugby School, an inquiry should be made whether the conditions of football at Rugby were not different from what they were elsewhere. The answer to this question, once formulated, is manifest. The conditions of football were different at Rugby from those which prevailed at other schools; or rather, to put the matter in language paradoxical in appearance but literally correct, the conditions of the game were normal at Rugby and abnormal everywhere else. In fact, the original form of football,—for it is the simplest,—is of such a nature that it can hardly be played except in a wide open space. Such a space existed at Rugby from the beginning, but not at the other great public schools. The Eton boys had originally no other place to disport themselves in than the comparatively small inner field nearest the

College buildings. The ancient Meads of the Winchester College are small in dimensions. At the Charterhouse they had originally no other play-ground than the cloisters; and though at Westminster the scholars were better provided for, yet they were confined to "Green." Now, in small spaces of this kind it is obvious that the continual playing of football throughout the winter months must, almost of necessity, have resulted in the ruin of the playground for other purposes. For football is essentially a game for the many, and not for the few, and by its very nature involves the tearing up of turf and the ruin of greenswards. Therefore it was natural that in each particular school the rules of the game should be settled by the capacities of the play-ground; and, as these were infinitely various in character, so were the games various.

It is proposed to examine the games of the various schools in somewhat close detail, on the ground, in the first place, that they are interesting in themselves, and, in the second, that in some of them at least are to be traced, more or less distinctly, the germs of the Association game.

The most peculiar of all games of football is that which is practised at Winchester, and which, in defiance of latter-day opinions, still continues to flourish in almost its pristine form. Of the peculiar rules in vogue at Winchester College, it cannot be written that they are in any way concerned with the principles of the Association game. On the contrary, they differ altogether from those of any other game. But the Winchester rules have the literary merit of peculiarity, and this practical virtue, that they have produced many of the first Association players of the present and past days. Therefore, although no one is recommended to submit himself to them if he can avoid it, which he will not be able to do if he goes to the ancient school as a pupil, they are rules worthy of some notice. The ground upon which the Winchester boys play, is about 80 yards long and about 25 yards wide. Thus, in the College Meads, which are more or less square, with an irregular excrescence upon the side nearest the College, it was possible for four games to be played simultaneously, while the central portion was reserved for the more sacred and elaborate game of cricket. Inasmuch, however, as there was some natural difficulty in keeping the ball within the prescribed limits for even a reasonable time, the ancient custom was first to mark out the ground with stakes and ropes, and then, outside the ropes, to place a line of shivering fags. In time humanity and genius combined discovered that hurdles served the purpose quite as well as small boys, and did not take cold; and in later days the hurdles themselves have given place to tarred nets, spread out upon an iron framework some ten feet in height. The ropes still remain and are placed about a yard from the netting; and further, seeing that the ball, while it is "under ropes," is in a certain spurious kind of way in play, these same ropes exert a serious influence upon the game. This commences with a "hot," which is formed in the following fashion : In "sixes," that is to say matches with six players on each side, there are two backs on each side, who are called "behinds," and four forwards, who go by the name of "ups." Of the forwards one is "over the ball" and takes the centre place, and two back him up with their knees behind his and their arms interlaced round his body. All three keep their heads down, and the fourth, with his back and shoulders, propels the centre man. In a six game, notwithstanding the closeness of the phalanx thus formed, the duration of a "hot" is not usually long; but in fifteens, where the mass of players is far greater and the same principle is observed in the formation of the "hot," ten minutes or more may be occupied in this performance. When it is added that the performance is deliberately repeated every time the ball is kicked over the netting, and that there is no other penalty than a "hot" for any infringement of the rules, it may be imagined that "hots" occupy the greater part of the hour which is devoted to a match. The ball, however, is not kicked out as often as might be supposed probable, for one of the most stringent rules of the game is, that it may not be kicked higher than five feet, which is supposed to be the average height of a man's shoulder, unless, at the time when it is kicked, it is either bounding or rolling at a distinctly fast pace; nor may it be kicked up unless the last person to touch it was an opponent, for, in the contrary case, it is a "made flier," which is dreadful. This is a rule which causes almost as many hots by being infringed as it saves by preventing the behinds, who alone do much in the way of kicking, from driving the ball over the netting. Still it is a necessary rule, for the goal consists of the whole twenty-five yards or thereabouts, that is to say, of the whole width of the arena, and but for the rule concerning "kicking up," there would be no end to the number of goals obtained. It should be mentioned, however, that if a ball, before passing over the goal line, or, as it is called,

"Worms," is touched ever so slightly by any member of what Strutt would call the defending party, no goal is scored. The distinguishing features of the game, apart from those already mentioned, are, in the first place, that no dribbling is permitted under any circumstances; and in the second place, that the "off-side" rule is stricter than in any other game. It is not legitimate for two players on the same side to touch the ball in succession, unless it rolls behind the first kicker; nor may one player "back up his partner's kick" by charging the adversary, unless, at the time when his partner kicked, he was behind the ball, or, since that time, has returned to the place from which the ball was kicked. It should be added, that the ball, which is several ounces heavier than an Association ball, is round. When caught upon a full volley kicked by one of the opposite side, it is "punted" and not "dropped;" but if the person catching it is charged, then he who charges is said to be "running him" and may "collar" him as at the Rugby game, and the holder of the ball may run until his adversaries cease to "run him," but then he must halt and take his punt.

Enough has now been said to give to the general public an idea of the Winchester game. To a Wykehamist, all that has been written is, as he

would say, the vilest "Tugs," or news twice told;
to interest him, it would be necessary to enter into
an elaborate discussion of the vexed question contained in the words "Under Ropes Play." But
to the outside world this vast problem will be
sufficiently explained by the bare statement that
when, towards the end of the allotted time, the
heavier side discovers that it is one goal or so
ahead, it is a very simple matter to keep the ball
under ropes, in the midst of a surging and
tumultuous crowd, until the hour ends.

The characteristics of the Winchester game are,
that it requires great pace and dash in the players,
and teaches men to kick with great accuracy. It
is, however, so manly and straightforward a game
that it leaves little room for skill or subtlety.
Moreover, it is noticeable for this, that while it has
been the training-ground of many excellent players,
it has also brought into prominence men who never
could have excelled under any other conditions.
These are the "under-ropes" players, whose system is that of the ox—heavy, obstinate, and slow.

Corresponding in a certain measure to the
Winchester game, is the Eton game of football at
the Wall. That is to say, its character and rules
are the result of the locality in which it is played.
This is a sturdy game, and a manly, but singularly

inappropriately termed football. The ball indeed and the feet are both present; but the ball is of miscroscopic size, the number of the players is considerable, and the limits of the ground are exceedingly narrow. Such is the compactness of the mass of players and the hardness of the wall alongside which the game takes place, that the ball is encased in a double covering, lest it should be burst; and the players are enveloped in a kind of armour of proof. If it were not for this precaution, minor excrescences, such as ears and the like, would be rubbed off as completely as jagged knobs are removed from a stick by sandpaper and spoke-shave; skin, too, would, at the end of the game, be conspicuous by its absence from the players nearest the wall.

Into the niceties of this game it is not proposed to enter; for though an excellent pastime, it cannot be described as football, and is simply a question of shoving. There used, however, to exist at Winchester College a practice not dissimilar. On Saturday evenings in the Christmas term, commonly called "short-half," it was customary for the College boys to assemble in 7th chamber for the purpose of singing; after the singing was over, the prefects assembled, eighteen in number, in the doorway, which was exceeding cramped; opposite

them the juniors, fifty-two in number, ranged themselves, and what was called a "down-hot" took
place. Juniors tried to force their way out, the
prefects tried to keep them in, and there was no
mercy for him who fell. With the single exception
that in a "down-hot" the formality of "delivering
a ball in the midst," as Strutt has it, was dispensed
with, there were many features of similarity
between it and the wall game. Lovers of football
might well wish that, as in life they were similar, so
in death they might not be divided. The "down-
hot," together with the College singing, has long
gone the way of all flesh, and has been swept into
the dustbin of the past by the broom of the
reformer.   It were a matter not much to be
regretted that the wall game should also perish.

The Eton field game, on the other hand, is a
very fine game of football, and has been found to
be an excellent training ground for Association.
Both in the forward and backward divisions old
Etonians have been prominent; and nothing but
the fact that personal references are contrary to our
principles prevents an enumeration of well-known
names.   The same deference to principle has pre-
vented the naming of Wykehamists who have been
heroes in international contests, and will prohibit
the mention of the names of the great players of

Harrow, of Westminster, of Rugby, and of Charter-house.

The distinguishing points of the field game are pace, and, if the word may be used without offence, honesty. The ball, as in the wall game, is very small, being about the size of a toy football such as one buys for children. It is also exceedingly light, and will travel at a great pace; the result is, that from the moment when they begin to play Eton boys volley without hesitation, and when they reach man's estate, can volley the Association ball incomparably better than the generality of men trained elsewhere. On the other hand, it is not, in our opinion, a good ball for men to play with. The full strength of a muscular leg, scientifically applied, drives the ball so far that there are periods at which either the game degenerates into an interchange of volleys between the backs ("behinds"), or the ball is occasionally kicked far beyond the reach of any player.

It now becomes necessary to explain the use of the word "honesty" a few lines above. There is no game, except perhaps the Winchester game, in which the rules of "off-side" are so strict; and to "corner" or to "sneak," that is to say, to play "off-side," or to hang about with the intention of so doing, are serious offences thoroughly foreign to the principle of the game.   Perhaps it is not too much to say, that in proportion to the strictness with which the off-side rule is formulated and observed is the normal pace of any game.   Certain it is, that of all games the Winchester, Eton, and Rugby games are the fastest, and that in them the off-side rule is most stringent.   The "bully" with which the Eton game begins, is very like a "scrimmage" or a "hot"; but there is this essential difference between the Eton game and the Winchester, that it permits and encourages dribbling; it differs from all games except the Association game in prohibiting the use of the hands; and from the Association game in particular, in the prohibition of forward passing. It should be mentioned that goals are not frequently obtained at this game, for the goal posts are both narrow and low; but there are minor points, called "rouges," which may be obtained, and which may score the victory.

A rouge is an intricate business; and it must be prefaced that the subjoined account is not written by an Etonian, who alone is familiar with the almost Eleusinian mystery, but is merely the result of something like a dozen experiences of the pleasant Eton game which used to be played in the Merton College cricket ground at Oxford.

The proceedings appeared to be these :—One side, which may be called A, having succeeded in driving the ball into the neighbourhood of the line running through B's goal from side to side of the ground, proceeded slowly to urge the ball along the line in the direction of the goal. In this performance they were carefully watched by their opponents, who did not interfere to prevent them unless one of the side A happened to lose command of the ball for a moment, for, if the ball was driven behind the line after last touching one of the side B, a rouge was scored to the credit of A. A rouge, besides being a point in itself, was capable of being turned into a goal; for when the ball had been driven behind, a peculiar and exceedingly compact scrimmage was formed close to the goal itself; one of the defending party holding the ball between his knees and sitting on the knee of a person behind him, who himself placed his foot upon the ball. These two principal defenders were themselves backed up by subordinates behind; and approach to them was rendered difficult by the arranging of a double line of players. Up the lane thus formed the opposing party, headed by their strongest and heaviest man, charged in column, at a heavy trot, and a tremendous struggle ensued.

The accuracy of this account of a rouge is not vouched for ; but it has at least this merit, that it is a faithful representation of the impression produced upon the mind of one not nurtured at Eton, by a few experiences of a most pleasant game.

The Harrow game, though nice enough in the playing, is neither fish, flesh, fowl, nor good red herring. It is played with a peculiarly awkward-looking oval ball, over which Harrow boys attain a complete mastery, but which completely gets the better of other players. Upon *à priori* grounds one would say that it was the most primitive form of ball, and originally represented nothing but a bladder with the rudest form of covering that could be put together out of three pieces of leather. The features of the game are the punting and the dribbling, and the fact that the goal has no limit in the way of height. *A solo usque ad cœlum*, in fact, is a maxim more applicable to the Harrow goal than, as may be seen from a recent decision in the matter of overhead wires, to territorial possession. The next most noticeable characteristic will be suggested immediately by the words " three yards." Any player may catch the ball on the full volley from a kick by one of the other side, or from a kick by one of his own side, if, at the time when the kick is made, he is nearer to his own goal than to that of the adversary. Having caught it he calls out " Three yards," making his mark in the ground with his heel, and if he does this in time, he is allowed a free kick at the adversaries' goal, no one being allowed to come within the distance named, for the purpose of interfering with his kick.

There are other games of football practised at various schools, which, in a work of more pretentious size, would deserve detailed description, besides those of Westminster and Charterhouse. There is, for instance, the Shrewsbury game, noted for its name of " dowling," supposed to be connected with δοῦλος, "a slave," which carries in itself the notion of compulsory football. But space does not permit us to enter into the merits of this game ; and the omission may be justified partly on the ground that it was a game of a mixed kind, and partly on the ground that it has now fallen into disuse, and has given place to the Association game.

Between the game as played in the cloisters at the Charterhouse, and that played on " Green " at Westminster School there would not appear to be any essential similarity. The rules of both games were absolutely determined by their environment

and the circumstances under which they were
played. In a certain sense, both were similar.
Both were played in a confined space, though, of
course, the space in "Green" was less confined
than that of the cloisters; and from this cause it
follows that both Westminster and Charterhouse
boys developed an astounding capacity for dribbling through dense masses of boys. Both games
again were played at odd times and in ordinary
clothes; and though both were rough and boister-
ous enough in all conscience, they clearly were not
so injurious to clothes as the Rugby game, in
which it was allowed to seize and hurl an opponent.
The worst that can follow from a charge in which
the hands are not employed, is downfall into mud
which a clothes-brush will remove more or less
completely from the injured garment; but from
being collared, there may ensue results in the
shape of torn clothes. Hence it came that the boys
educated at these schools, in the first place, pro-
hibited "collaring" and all use of the hands and
arms, and, in the second place, became extremely
clever at dribbling and at charging with the
shoulders. While this subject is uppermost, it
may not be amiss to enter very slightly into the
question of roughness. The Rugby game unquestionably appears far rougher to the spectator than

the Association.   But, in fact, it is a very doubtful matter which is the more dangerous.   It must be remembered that it is not the fall to the ground which is most perilous to life and limb.   Seldom, indeed, is it that anything more serious than a collar-bone is broken by a fall to the ground. From the concussion of two bodies, on the contrary, ribs and arms are apt to suffer, and in proportion to the preponderance of kicking is the danger of broken legs.   These are of comparatively rare occurrence, except as the results of crossed shins ; and the more rational conclusion is, that the rules from which the Association game took its origin were originally formulated, or rather grew naturally, from a regard for clothes rather than limbs.

In another chapter the formulation of the Association Rules will be discussed; for the present, it will be enough to say that they owe their origin mostly to Westminster and Charterhouse.   Indeed, it is not too much to say of the games of football at present in vogue, that they are due almost entirely to the desire of men at the Universities and elsewhere for a continuance of their old school exercises, and that their connection with the ancient games is accidental rather than real, remote rather than near.

Of the history of the other form of the game, in which running with the ball is encouraged, but little need be said ; for from Rugby School, and from Rugby School alone, what is now known as the Rugby Union game is derived.

. If the view we have taken in the foregoing pages be correct, while the running and collaring game was the original national sport of England, the dribbling game owes its origin to schools in which the playgrounds were limited in size, and where various considerations rendered the rough horseplay which characterized football in the ancient times impracticable. In the beginning of this chapter we have pointed out that the size of the Close at Rugby rendered it possible for the boys of that school to play the original game without fear of being hurled when collared against stone walls, or iron railings, or upon surfaces of gravel. Hence we should naturally expect to find, in the game practised at this school, an absence of any restriction in the way in which the ball was to be taken towards the adversaries' goal, and an equal absence of any restriction in the means of collaring or stopping one of the attacking party in his course, and with no limits to the field of play except those which necessity demanded. It is the very style of game which is known to have been in vogue at Rugby fifty years ago. We need scarcely refer to the well-known description of the football match in "Tom Brown's Schooldays at Rugby," as that description is hardly likely to be unknown to any of our readers ; but if any take the trouble to reperuse it after reading these pages, they can scarcely fail to notice how little the Rugby game described there differs from a Rugby Union " Big-side " at the present day. Indeed, until within the last few years the Rugby School game suffered no alteration ; but lately the tripping, hacking, and indiscriminate charging have been abandoned, no doubt more in respect to the feelings of the numerous fifteens who visit the school to play matches, than from any assumed effeminacy of the hard-shinned Rugbeians. At the present day we believe the Rugby School fifteens, at any rate in their foreign matches, conform to the Rugby Union Code.

No doubt there were many other schools at which a game which allowed running with the ball was practised ; but at no other public school than Rugby, as far as we are aware, did the collaring, hacking, and tripping game take root. We can hardly help thinking, when we recollect with what rapturous delight football was regarded at Rugby, that the real cause which kept Rugby football in the background in other schools, was the sublunary consideration of clothes. In ancient times a suit of clothes was an expensive item of expenditure for a young gentleman, while the beef and mutton that he ate cost but a few pence the pound; and so in every sport the question of how the clothes would stand it had to be considered. Had Carlyle been still alive, we might have provided him with materials for another chapter of *Sartor Resartus.*

CONCLUSION.

The Modern Revival of Football.

A VERY useful rule forbids an historian to deal with the matters of his own day; and in obedience to this rule we have decided not to discuss the developments, changes, and general progress of modern football since the institution of the governing bodies of the two games—Association and Rugby Union—placed each of them upon a firm basis as a national sport. The only task, therefore, left to us before we conclude our welcome labours, is to sketch in outline the steps which led to the re-establishment of football in its old position as the chief of the winter sports of England.

Between thirty and forty years ago began the first movement in England of the great athletic revival, which, after gradually spreading until it covered the whole of the United Kingdom, is still rolling like a wave over the colonies and all foreign countries where the English tongue is spoken. It will not be too much for us to say, that the great athletic movement, which is still too near for us to be able to calculate its full effects with certainty, has worked a greater revolution in English character and habits than any movement, religious or secular, which has passed over the country since the time of the Puritans. Of that great athletic movement the history has yet to be written ; but it would hardly be wise to attempt to touch it in the present work. Suffice it to say, that the physical causes of the desire for hard exercise which has seized upon men are apparent enough. In modern times, when nearly all the world is given up to the feverish bustle and worry of money-making, the body of a young and lusty man, by a natural reaction, craves for a muscular exercise, which may give a relief to the nerves and the brain. For the performance of this function it is admitted that there is no game in the world like football. The student at the University, and the young man who is tied to his office-stool throughout all the daylight hours of the winter months, with the solitary boon of a Saturday's half-holiday, alike find that an hour's hustle at football sends them home, more tired perhaps, but happier, calmer, and wiser men.

It is no doubt in some sense owing to the promptings of this feeling that we find, about thirty years ago, football-playing being revived fitfully at the Universities, and matches beginning to be played between teams of men in London and the provinces, and with still greater frequency as years went by. In 1857 the Sheffield Club (Association) was founded, and in 1858 the great metropolitan Rugby Union Club, Blackheath, was established, chiefly by some old pupils of Blackheath School. About 1861 or 1862 a large number of clubs playing the dribbling game sprang up in the neighbourhood of Sheffield, which has since remained a most flourishing local centre for that game ; while in London two of the first clubs who started the dribbling game were the Crystal Palace, in 1861, and the Barnes Club, in 1862. Indeed, at this time the number and organization of the dribbling clubs, both in London and the provinces, was superior to those of the advocates of the running and tackling game. As far as we are aware, the Blackheath Club was the only regularly organized club in the metropolis until the great rival club at Richmond came into existence, in 1862. It is in 1863 that the history of football organization really commences. In the autumn of that year a conference met for the purpose of attempting to reduce to a uniform code the various conflicting rules which were adopted by the different clubs. It was the intention of the promoters of the meeting to unite all those who played football under any rules into a united body; and the rules agreed upon at the first meeting were a fair and liberal attempt to bring about what can hardly be considered anything but an impossible task, viz., a fusion of Rugby Union and Association rules. Indeed, the original rules, framed by the promoters of the parent Association, included running with the ball under certain restrictions, as well as hacking and tripping. In the meantime, however, another conference of members of the public schools had been arranging rules at Cambridge, where the dribbling game had been played on Parker's Piece as early as 1855. Eventually, a meeting was arranged between delegates of the Cambridge and London conferences; and between them a set of rules was agreed to which excluded all running with the ball, and all tackling, hacking, or tripping. Thus started in 1863 the Football Association; and, save that in 1867 the strict off-side rule, which was at first insisted upon, was expunged for the present modified rule, which gives rise to so many disputes, there have been few substantial alterations in the rules up to the present day, though many changes in the manner of playing. . After this alteration the players from Westminster and Charterhouse Schools joined the Association ranks; and in 1870 the sixteen clubs which formed the Sheffield Association abandoned their own rules in favour of those of the Association, which has from that day exercised paramount authority over all the dribbling clubs of the kingdom. At the present moment the popularity of the Association game, especially in the provinces, is enormous; and if the old governing body can stand firm amidst the troubles which are arising at the present day upon the vexed question of professionalism, its career of prosperity should be a long one.

To return, however, to the history of the running and tackling form of the sport—the "Rugby game," as it was called even it 1862. When the Association code forbade running with the ball, the Blackheath and Richmond Clubs, and the few other less important and scarcely permanent teams who played the running rules, naturally held aloof from the Associated clubs. In the meantime the number of permanent clubs who played Rugby rules began to multiply greatly. In 1863 the Civil Service Club, under, these rules, was formed, and .about the same time the Harlequins. In 1865

Ravenscourt Park was founded; in 1866 the
Flamingoes in London, and several provincial
clubs, including Liverpool; and between this time
and 1870 the clubs playing the older game sprang
up in large numbers all over the kingdom. Although there was a general similarity in all the
rules played by the various clubs who admitted
running and tackling into their game, the difficulty
of arranging little disputes and differences of
practice used to be very great, as all old players
who had their day before the foundation of the
Rugby Union in 1871 can testify.   Disputes of
any consequence were avoided by the universal
adoption of the rule that every club played its own
rules in home matches.   It was evident, however,
that a system like this could not last amidst the
rapid spread of the game through the country,
and in the autumn of 1870 negotiations commenced between members of the Blackheath and
Richmond Clubs, which ended, in January, 1871,
in the foundation of the Rugby Union.   It is
pleasing to note that the two governing bodies of
football have never come into collision since their
respective foundations.   We venture to express a
hope that the footballers of either game will ever
continue to look upon skill in the other and rival
game with admiration, and not with envy.

Recent Books

AND

Something About Them

London :

FIELD & TUER, THE LEADENHALL PRESS,
50, LEADENHALL STREET, E.C.

∞ INDEX ∞

Recent Books & Something About Them.

Chap-book Chaplets : Adorn'd with suitable

Sculptures by JOSEPH CRAWHALL. *The many hundreds of cuts being all hand-coloured, the issue is necessarily limited.* Contents of the Volume: I.—The Barkshire Lady's Garland. II.—The Babes in the Wood. III.—I know what I know. IV.—Jemmy and Nancy of Yarmouth. V.—The Taming of a Shrew. VI.—Blew-cap for me. VII.—John and Joan. VIII.—George Barnwell. LONDON: Field & Tuer, The Leadenhall Press, E.C.

[In one thick 4to Volume, Twenty-five Shillings.

A REPRODUCTION in facsimile of the crudely printed and often humorously illustrated pamphlets that were hawked about the country by the chapmen of a bygone age. Book collectors, antiquarians, and lovers of the quaint and curious will be charmed with the reproduction in volume form of the literature that amused the leisure hours of their forefathers. From first to last the tales are literally crowded with amusing and characteristic cuts, all hand-coloured. The type, though purposely thick and coarse, is very legible, while the illustrations, charming in their unique humour, will provoke smiles from the gravest.

Olde ffrendes wyth newe Faces : Adorn'd

with suitable Sculptures by JOSEPH CRAWHALL. *The many hundreds of cuts being all hand-coloured, the issue is necessarily limited.* Table of the matter herein contained : I.—The louing Ballad of Lord Bateman. II.—A true relation of the Apparition of Mrs. Veal. III.—The Long Pack: A Northumbrian Tale. IV.—The Sword Dancers. V —John Cunningham, the Pastoral Poet. VI.—Ducks and Green Peas, or the Newcastle Rider : a Tale in Rhyme. VII.—Ducks and Green Peas : a Farce. VIII.—Andrew Robinson Stoney Bowes, Esq. IX.— The Gloamin' Buchte. LONDON : Field & Tuer, The Leadenhall Press, E.C. [In one thick 4to Volume, Twenty-five Shillings.

THE description appended to "Chapbook Chaplets " applies equally to "Olde ffrendes."

✦ The ✦ Leadenhall ✦ Press ✦

LONDON, S.C.

Recent Books & Something About Them.

Recent Books &
Something About Them.

Recent Books &
Something About Them.

Recent Books & Something About Them.

❦ POETRY ❦

" An elegant birthday or New Year's gift."

Love Letters. By a Violinist. Consisting

of Twelve Letters on the Despair, the Hope, and the Victory of this True Lover, inclusive of his Confessions and his Vision of Beethoven, together with other matters of interest. Printed on antique paper, bound in vellum and tied with old gold silken strings. LONDON: Field & Tuer, The Leadenhall Press, E.C.   [Seven-and-Sixpence.

A COLLECTION of poems setting forth the eulogies of love, music, and fidelity. The collection is divided into twelve parts, each being a lyric or letter addressed to a beautiful and accomplished lady. The arrangement of the lines constitutes what may be considered a new metre.

" As the brightest of poets have passed away,
Now it's left between Tennyson and James Gay."

Canada's Poet: By "Yours alway, James Gay"

(Of the Royal City of Guelph, Ontario), Poet Laureate of Canada, and Master of all Poets. LONDON : Field & Tuer, The Leadenhall Press, E.C. " As amusing as English as She is Spoke."   [One Shilling.

T HE *Saturday Review* has treated "Canada's Poet" as the "thinnest" joke of the generation. But the fact is this amusing book is not a joke at all. The whole point of its publication is, that like "English as She is Spoke," it is a serious book, seriously written, and its author, James Gay, is serious in believing himself to be on a level with Lord Tennyson, to whom it will be observed his " poems " are affectionately dedicated.

My Ladye and Others: Poems: Satirical,

Philosophical, and Arcadian : By J. W. GILBART-SMITH, B.A., Christ Church, Oxon. Second Edition. LONDON: Field & Tuer, The Leadenhall Press, E.C.   [Ten-and-Sixpence.

A SERIES of charmingly written society verses.

✤ The ✤ Leadenhall ✤ Press ✤

LONDON, S.C.

"

Recent Books &
Something About Them.

⊶ FICTION ⊷

"An absurdly amusing book. There are hearty laughs in it."—*Judy*.

Holy Blue! By Alphonse de Florian (tra-

duced into the English by Himself). With an Introduction by JAMES
MILLINGTON. LONDON: Field & Tuer, The Leadenhall Press, E.C.
[Two-and-Sixpence; cloth, Three-and-Sixpence.

AN amusingly egotistical quasi-biographical story, written in
idiomatic French and literally translated into the English
language by the author—one of the Frenchiest of French writers.

"An interesting and cleverly written novel by a new author."

This Year, Next Year, Sometime, Never. A

Novel, by PUCK. LONDON: Field & Tuer, The Leadenhall
Press, E.C. [In Two Volumes, One Guinea.

A STORY of to-day and of people one constantly meets.
Though non-sensational in the sense of not dealing with
hair-breadth escapes and striking situations, the interest of a
remarkable and well told story is maintained throughout.

(PRINCE PERTINAX : *see* ILLUSTRATED.)

❋ MISCELLANEOUS ❋

"Far more piquant and amusing even than 'John Bull and his Island,' to
which it is the companion volume."

John Bull's Womankind. By Max O'Rell,

Author of "John Bull and His Island." First Edition, Twenty-five
Thousand. LONDON: Field & Tuer, The Leadenhall Press, E.C.
[Yellow Covers, Two-and-Sixpence; Cloth, Three-and-Sixpence.

IN this volume, which is the continuation of "John Bull and
his Island," Max O'Rell describes, in his happiest vein of
wit and humour, the domestic side of English women, London
beauties, shop girls, actresses, women's rights, hallelujah lasses,
and so forth.

Recent Books &
Something About Them.

Recent Books &
Something About Them.

Tree Gossip. By Francis George Heath.
LONDON : Field & Tuer, The Leadenhall Press, E.C.   [3s. 6d.

A BOOK on the oddities, mainly, of tree life, and one that, taking the reader into the byways of tree lore, gives interesting facts not usually found in books on trees. Its aim is to discuss its subject lightly and pleasantly, so that whilst it communicates little-known matters it endeavours to do this in the form of entertaining " Gossip."

"An excellent manual."—Athenæum.

An Essay of Scarabs: By W. J. Loftie, B.A.,
F.S.A. (Author of " A History of London ") together with a Catalogue of Ancient Egyptian Amulets of various kinds, bearing the names of Kings. LONDON : Field & Tuer, The Leadenhall Press, E.C.
[Twenty-one Shillings.

C ONTAINS an account of the use of the *Scarabæus*, or beetle, as an amulet by the ancient Egyptians, to whom the animal and its image in stone or pottery were significant of the resurrection. To the essay is appended the illustrated catalogue of an extensive and valuable collection of these curious objects bearing the names of Egyptian kings, and standing to history in the same relation as a collection of coins. One hundred and twenty (numbered) copies only have been printed, of which only a small number remain unsold.

"A quaint little volume."—Pall Mall Gazette.

Ye Oldest Diarie of Englysshe Travell: Being
the hitherto unpublished narrative of the pilgrimage of Sir Richard Torkington to Jerusalem in 1517. Edited by W. J. LOFTIE, B.A., F.S.A. Author of " A History of London," &c., &c. LONDON: Field & Tuer, The Leadenhall Press, E.C.
[One Shilling.

T HE amusement to be derived from reading these ancient travels, and guessing at the curiously misspelt names is almost endless. After the title was chosen and printed it was found that a nearly contemporary diary, that of Guylforde, had already been circulated by a literary society ; but, as Torkington went over nearly the same ground only a few years later, and as his narrative is much more personal, and more amusing and quaintly told it has not been thought necessary to make any alteration.

✦ The ✦ Leadenhall ✦ Press ✦

LONDON, E.C.

(17)

Recent Books & Something About Them.

Recent Books & Something About Them.

Recent Books & Something About Them.

Recent Books &
Something About Them.

The Opening of China. Six Letters reprinted

from *The Times* on the present condition and future prospects of China. By A. R. COLQUHOUN, Assoc. Mem. Inst. C.E., F.R.G.S., Author of "Across Chrysê," etc., Special Correspondent of *The Times* in China. With an Introduction by S. H. LOUTTIT. LONDON: Field & Tuer, The Leadenhall Press, E.C.   [One Shilling.

A N exhaustive account of the present condition of China, and suggesting means for the opening of that Empire to European commerce.

LORD BEACONSFIELD ON THE CONSTITUTION.

"What is he?" and "A Vindication of the English Constitution." By "Disraeli the Younger."

[The Earl of Beaconsfield, K.G.] Edited with an anecdotical preface by FRANCIS HITCHMAN, author of "The Public Life of the Earl of Beaconsfield," &c. LONDON: Field & Tuer, The Leadenhall Press, E.C.   [Two-and-Sixpence.

THE only vindicator of the "lost leader" of the Tories that is necessary. A reprint of the famous and long lost pamphlet "What is he?" of which it is believed that only one copy is in existence, and of the almost equally scarce "Vindication of the Constitution," which Disraeli the Younger addressed to Lord Lyndhurst in 1835. The former establishes the identity of Disraeli's politics in youth and in age, and the latter vindicates the consistency of the two great men with whose names it is associated against the calumnies of Lord Campbell. Mr. Hitchman's preface contains a great number of highly interesting and hitherto unpublished facts concerning the Disraeli family.

"Novel readers and novel writers may advantageously study its pages."
Ethics of Some Modern Novels: By Trevor

CREIGHTON. LONDON: Field & Tuer, The Leadenhall Press, E.C.
[One Shilling.

A BRIEF review of the morals of some of the more notable novels of the day, in which the author plainly says that vice is too apt to be surrounded by a halo of sentimentalism, and that the line is not clearly marked between right and wrong.

+ The + Leadenhall + Press +

LONDON, E.C.

Recent Books &
Something About Them.

Dickens Memento (with Introductions by

FRANCIS PHILLIMORE and JOHN F. DEXTER.) Catalogue, with purchasers' names and prices realised, of the pictures, drawings, and objects of art of the late Charles Dickens, dispersed at Christie, Manson & Woods in 1870. LONDON: Field & Tuer, The Leadenhall Press, E.C.

A BEAUTIFULLY printed and luxuriously got-up book of special value to the Dickens collector. In three separate divisions, the text includes primarily a reprint of the catalogue of the Dickens sale, at which it may be remembered almost fabulous sums were realised. Mr. Francis Phillimore contributes a gossipy and interesting introduction, and Mr. John F. Dexter a lengthy, learned, and exhaustive paper on book rarities, subtitled "Hints to Dickens Collectors."

Bewick Memento (with an Introduction by

ROBERT ROBINSON). Catalogue, with purchasers' names and prices realised, of the scarce and curious collection of silver plate, prints, pictures, wood blocks, copperplates, and Bewick relics, &c., dispersed at Newcastle-upon-Tyne in 1884. Illustrated. LONDON: Field & Tuer, The Leadenhall Press, E.C.

A BEAUTIFULLY printed and luxuriously got-up book of special value to the Bewick collector. Mr. Robert Robinson, of Newcastle-upon-Tyne, who contributes the introduction, has been connected during the greater part of a long lifetime with the Bewick family, and he writes with a full knowledge of his subject. Of the eighteen beautiful illustrations, printed on separate leaves, twelve embellished the original catalogue, but the six additional at the end, including the humorously treated frontispiece of "Cows Angling"—all charming specimens of Bewick's skill with the graver—are first impressions from blocks hitherto not printed from.

"By far the most complete, and at the same time entertaining book on old glass yet published."—*Saturday Review*.

Glass in the Old World: By M. A. Wallace-

DUNLOP. With Illustrations. LONDON: Field & Tuer, The Leadenhall Press, E.C.   [Twelve-and-Sixpence.

A MOST comprehensive and entertaining epitome of what is known about glass in ancient times and in all countries. A treasury of information full of interest and anecdote.

+ The + Leadenhall + Press +

LONDON, E.C.

Recent Books &
Something About Them.

Recent Books &
Something About Them.

www.ingramcontent.com/pod-product-compliance
Lightning Source LLC
Chambersburg PA
CBHW060958050726

47592CB00003B/1256